recovering from depression

a guide to overcoming your self sabotaging tendencies and learning healthy coping mechanisms

MAGGIE KELLY

Recovering from Depression © Copyright 2022 Maggie Kelly

For more information, email maggie@maggiepkelly.com.

ISBN (paperback): 979-8-88759-245-9

ISBN (eBook): 979-8-88759-246-6

Download the FREE Journaling Prompts!

To get the best experience with this book, download the prompts here: 50 Self-Reflective Journaling Prompts. With this, you will be equipped to process and heal in your journey more efficiently.

You can get a copy by visiting:

www.maggiepkelly.com

Table of Contents

Introduction

Getting help is difficult. You don't want to admit there's a problem, because then it means you have to change. And change is hard.

Getting help requires changing your sense of identity and losing a part of it. For a long time, I thought I would always be "depressed." It wasn't until after my stay in the mental hospital that I thought I could live without depression.

You're going to be sad about this. That's normal. You're mourning a part of yourself. You need to say goodbye to it, but that doesn't change the fact that it was still a part of you.

That's what this book is about. And if you've got here, I'm so proud of you. I'm so proud of you for taking the first step in your recovery. It takes guts.

It is by no means easy to reach out for help. You will resist. However, once you push past the resistance, you will open yourself up to a brighter future.

You're struggling and you don't know what to do. You feel lost, trying to find your place in the world.

You're convinced that your mental illness is going to take you out. You're convinced you're going to die, that you're not making it out of this war alive.

It feels like it's the end of the world and you're going down. You keep thinking this is your life and nothing is ever going to change. You're going to be stuck feeling this way forever.

I see you. I used to be exactly like you.

I started struggling with depression when I was 13. It was horrible. It followed me around for years, clinging to me like a backpack.

I couldn't get rid of it. There were seasons of my life that brought me down to my knees with depression. There were periods of my life when I could barely drag myself out of bed. But I still got up, every day.

I knew there was more to life. I couldn't feel this way forever. This couldn't be my life. I was determined to climb out of the hole depression had thrown me in.

I did it. And now, I want to show you *how* I did it.

A Personal Congratulations

You've just made your first positive choice.

You woke up today, alive, and you're reading this. That's amazing. The fact that you are reading this shows how strong you are.

You picked up this book because you want help. Just now, you've empowered yourself to make positive choices in the name of mental health.

Now that you have that help, I'm here to tell you: you're okay.

Not only that, but you're a survivor. A fighter. A warrior.

Living is one of the hardest things you have to do, and you're doing it. This life is not easy, but you're getting through it, day by day.

Every day you manage to get through is another day you get to put in your "win" column. It's another day that you beat your mental illness. Congratulations on making it to today.

You Have the Mental Fortitude

You've put up with the worst of the worst—your own thoughts. They keep coming after you, trying to get you down. Sometimes, they succeed…but sometimes, they don't. And that's key. They haven't won.

For a long time, I thought things like:

-   I'm a burden

-   I don't matter to anyone

- The world would be better off without me

You've been fighting a battle against thoughts like these for a long time now. While the end may not be in sight, you do have the strength to get there.

All the bad thoughts you've had so far, you've been able to combat. Every single one of them. The darkness continues to threaten to take over, but every day you make it out alive, you're winning.

Right now, you're stuck in tunnel vision. You're driving through the tunnel, and all you see is darkness. The tunnel is so long, you can't see through to the light on the other side. You may not be able to see the light, but know it's there.

You're stuck in your depression. The darkness is all-encompassing, but you know there has to be something better.

Hang on to that hope. The dark tunnel isn't going to last forever.

The Bad Days Won't Win

"You've made it through 100% of your bad days." —Norm Kelly

Depression will drag you to the depths of Tartarus and make you feel like you'll never get out. It feels like you've been stripped of your will to live.

You have already made it through all the most difficult things in your life. You can get through this, too.

In college, I used to count down the hours and minutes, waiting for them to pass by. I wasn't counting down to anything particular. Counting the time was a way for me to get through. "Getting through" was my one and only focus.

Every time you thought you wouldn't make it, you came out on the other side. You've battled your worst days and got through them. You can get through the rest of them, too.

The One Constant You Can Count On

The one constant of the world is change. If there's one thing you can count on, it's that nothing stays the same.

You may feel hopeless now. But you won't always feel this way. Feelings change, if you give them time. Feelings don't stay the same. In fact, nothing stays the same.

There is nothing you can count on in the world. There are no guarantees in life. The only two guarantees are that life will change and, eventually, you will die.

There's no need to speed up the timeframe of your life. You can find joy in your life. Depression doesn't have to rule your life.

Take it from me. After years of struggling with my mental disorder, I got help. It took hitting rock bottom before I got there, but I did get there.

I was hospitalized in the winter of 2020. I spent two months in the mental hospital, dying for someone to listen to my pleas for help. And, one day, a person came into my life and changed it forever.

I got electroconvulsive therapy (ECT) and went through the wringer of recovery. I got a psychiatrist and therapist that served my needs. After months of doing the work, I found joy in my life again by realizing that I had to embrace change.

I'm so glad you've stuck around this far. The world is far brighter with you in it. Thank you for being here and for staying alive.

Don't wait any longer to get better. Don't wait for your illness to get worse before you can get better. Don't wait until it's too late. You don't have to hit rock bottom. You can get better *now*. All you have to do is keep reading.

Section 1

Understanding Your
Mental Health

Chapter 1

The Health Connection

I've struggled with depression since I was 13, for well over a decade. Depression has always been there, lurking in the background, but some times were worse than others.

It became particularly rough after my dad got sick. He was diagnosed with lung cancer in the beginning of 2015. My dad resisted and refused to accept he was dying, and it put strain on our family.

I had a good relationship with my dad, but as he got sicker, our relationship strained. His poor health was reflected in ours, especially mentally.

After he died in 2016, I was gearing up to complete my final year of college. My last semester, I took 22 credit hours, including my senior thesis. To say I was stressed is an understatement. Mentally, I still couldn't fathom that my dad was dead. Socially, I was isolated. And physically, I was stiff like a log.

One night, I was reading *The Miracle Morning*, a book by Hal Elrod. He engineered the perfect morning routine that allowed you to spend time on personal development every day. The idea of having a morning routine was compelling. Something clicked in my mind.

I always wanted to run, but had never tried doing it. The following day, I put on my shoes and went for my first run. It cleared my mind and gave me an energy boost. Running gave me a way to cope, and it made me feel better in nearly every way.

Even on early days, I made it a point to go for a quick run before heading off to my classes. I ended my senior year getting all As and landing on the President's List.

The more I ran, the more invested I became in my health. Eventually, it led me to learning concepts like the health triangle.

The Health Triangle

The health triangle is an overview of your health, divided into three parts: physical, mental, and social.

Physical health refers to how well your body functions. It consists of activities such as exercising, eating healthy, and sleeping well.

Mental Health refers to your thoughts, feelings, and emotions. Being mentally healthy means being able to balance these, as well as strengthening your ability to cope with stress.

Social health refers to our relationships with others, whether it's family, friends, or coworkers.

All three are connected. It's important to maintain a balance, because if one suffers, they all suffer. After all, most people don't realize that their mind and body are connected more closely than anything else.

The Mind-Body Connection

The mind-body connection is the feedback loop between your mental and physical health. The mind-body connection says the two are not separate entities. Each mind and body pair affect each other. For example, when you feel anxious, your heart rate goes up and your body becomes more alert.

Your mind can affect how healthy your body is, and what you do with your physical body can impact your mental state.

This means the way you feel influences the way you think, and vice versa.

"The brain and peripheral nervous system, the endocrine and immune systems, and indeed, all the organs of our body and all the emotional responses we have, share a common chemical language and are constantly communicating with one another."—Dr. James Gordon ("What Is the Mind-Body Connection?" Taking Charge of Your Health & Wellbeing. Accessed October 9, 2022. https://www.takingcharge.csh.umn.edu/what-is-the-mind-body-connection.)

It's important to note that "mind" is not synonymous with "brain." Your mind consists of your mental states, like your thoughts, emotions, beliefs, and attitudes. Your brain is "the hardware that allows us to experience these mental states," as Dr. Jennifer Weinberg explains. (Monroe, Jamison. "Understanding the Mind-Body Connection." Newport Academy. Newport Academy, October 6, 2022. https://www.newportacademy.com/resources/mental-health/understanding-the-mind-body-connection/)

Think of it like a computer. Your brain is the computer's hardware, all the physical parts that house the internal parts and processes, including the mind—which is like a computer's software.

The mind-body connection plays an important part in the treatment of mental health. Since your physical and mental health are connected, if you improve one, you can improve the other.

Take yoga and meditation, for example. They are physical actions that impact the brain by calming the Central Nervous System (CNS). Yoga and meditation are practices of being mindful of your body. With yoga and meditation, you focus on what you *can* control.

I've found yoga and meditation to be calming. When I can spend a few minutes breathing deep and meditating, the rest of my body soon regulates and relaxes, and my mind usually follows.

However, it is hard to know the extent to which the mind controls the body. This can be even harder when there's a feedback loop.

The Feedback Loop

A feedback loop is a process in which the outputs of a system are circled back and used as inputs.

Poor mental health often leads to poor physical health, and vice versa. Your mental state determines your ability to move, and your ability to move affects your physical health.

When your mental health is suffering, chances are you aren't bouncing around the walls and running marathons or doing anything to physically help your mental health. And if your energy levels are low, then you have lower motivation, making it hard to mentally motivate yourself to improve your physical health.

Poor mental health can lead to chronic diseases, such as diabetes, asthma, cancer, cardiovascular disease, and arthritis.

If you aren't exercising, you're more susceptible to mental illness. Your body isn't releasing the necessary hormones that help you feel good and regulate your mood, so your mental health is at risk. On days where I sit inside, watch Netflix, and eat junk food, my mental health is significantly worse than on days when I exercise.

Below are some other factors that can also create negative feedback loops in your body:

- If you don't sleep well, then you likely will have physical discomfort, which leads to mental health problems. It doesn't matter which comes first—poor sleep or mental health problems. Once one starts, the other degrades. These problems feed into each other and create a never-ending loop.

- People with mental illness are more likely to develop smoking addictions. Your mental illness affects your dopamine levels and keeps them from releasing. When your body doesn't release dopamine, it ruins your mood and lowers your energy. Smoking releases that dopamine and makes you feel good, but this will only cause more health problems later down the line, which in turn will negatively affect your mental health, and so on.

- When I feel bad about myself or have bad mental health days, I don't want to do anything. It's easy to take a backseat approach and do nothing. And when I do nothing, I continue to feel worse, fueling the cycle.

With these loops in mind, you can become more aware of your thoughts and actions. Once you become aware of one of these loops taking place, you can do something to change it. I was able to use awareness of these loops to challenge my depression by sticking to running, even when my mind told me to stop and give up.

In Summary

Your physical, mental, and emotional health make up the three sides of the health triangle. Your physical and mental health have a distinct impression on each other, called the mind-body connection. Your health creates a loop that feeds back into itself.

Next: How our view of mental health leads to dysfunction in society

Chapter 2

High-Functioning Mental Illness is Ruining Our Society

It was the first year of college and I was in my dorm room. I opened my Facebook feed and saw posts littering my feed, all saying the same thing:

R.I.P, Dead, Deceased, We'll miss you.

My heart stopped. *What the hell?* As I read, I came to understand the horrifying conclusion. One of my high school classmates was dead. More specifically, he committed suicide.

He was only 18, and a senior in high school. He had his whole life to look forward to. It left everyone in a state of shock. Nobody saw it coming.

He was one of the happiest, funniest guys in class. There was no way he could have had depression like me.

Right?

Hiding In Plain Sight

Does this sound familiar to anyone? It's not uncommon for people to lose a loved one and have no clue they were even struggling to begin with.

You expect that someone's external expressions match their internal states. Someone appears happy on the outside, so you assume they're happy on the inside, too. What do you picture when you hear the word, "depressed?"

You probably picture people looking blue and lonely. People who have been isolated in their homes, living secluded. They lie in bed all day, huddled up underneath the covers.

While depression can look like this, it usually looks completely different. In reality, a person with depression looks just like you and me. It's because there isn't one "look" when it comes to mental illnesses. Mental illnesses hide in plain sight.

Depression looks like your friends, your neighbors, and your coworkers. People across the world struggle with their mental health, but there is no one "look" to keep an eye out for. I always presented a strong front to others, but it didn't stop the heavy weight inside my chest.

Often, depression is hidden. Your friend is feigning a smile, but on the inside they feel like they're dying.

Uncomfortable with Depression

The reason people still have these outdated pictures of what depression looks like is because no one wants to talk about depression. When it comes to mental health, sometimes it's like we're still living in the dark ages. It's uncommon to talk about your feelings. Generally, you're told not to feel your feelings.

We live around this narrative that feelings are for fools and one *must* be strong, no matter how they feel.

This is a damaging and harmful narrative, but it's a part of our society. It lives with us, inside us, and it's perpetuated in our beliefs and how we behave.

It's the belief that "*Boys don't cry,*" and "*Girls are too emotional.*"

Internally, you're taught to not feel. Feelings make you weak. Feelings make you spineless. You are told you can't be strong and have feelings.

You're not supposed to feel, so you minimize your internal states. You blow them off, thinking they don't matter.

Nowadays, you struggle with the fact that you don't want to feel. You struggle to turn your emotions off, but you just can't. You want to get it out, talk about it, get it off your chest, but when you do, you're judged or feel like you are failing at doing it "right."

I was criticized for being too emotional, so I learned to repress my emotions. I kept my feelings inside for the comfort of others, and it nearly killed me.

Expressing your feelings might as well make you a leper.

All of this only propagates the problem.

Just like the feedback loop, you keeping it in, letting the emotions fester, will one day result in you blowing up.

You could avoid the blow-up altogether if it weren't taboo to talk about mental health.

Recognizing Mental Health

Talking is the first step to learning what depression actually looks like. If you're like me, then you know what it's like to have depression. You know what it's like to get up every day and go about your life.

This type of depression is labeled "high-functioning," as if the mere presence of a mental disorder usually means you can't function. High-functioning refers to how a person seemingly functions perfectly on the outside.

It's talked about as if one version of mental distress is better than the other. "At least you can get out of bed and go to work, right?" That's what I imagine society has to say to those of us with high-functioning depression. They see us as the lucky ones who don't have to fear their mental health. As if the only way your mental illness is valid is if it incapacitates you.

Your body was made to withstand hurricanes, earthquakes, and typhoons. It can survive a few bad emotions. It seems like your depression is not a big deal so long as you aren't incapacitated.

However, despite what others may think, my depression is real and my depression is painful, even when I can manage to take care of myself. Just because I get up and get to work on time doesn't mean my depression doesn't exist, or that I'm not struggling.

Everyone is hurting in their own way. You can't tell by looking at people, and that's the point. You don't know based on someone's appearance whether they're depressed or not.

Depression doesn't have a look. It comes in all shapes and sizes.

If we want people to understand, we have to start openly discussing mental health. We have to stop pretending it isn't real. We have to allow people to feel.

Rates of depression and anxiety are increasing worldwide. Given the state of the world, it's no surprise. This growth should, if anything, blow the doors of conversation wide open. Once I sought help and opened up about my trials, it lifted a weight off my shoulders. It could do the same for you, as well.

Depression hides underneath the surface. It festers, waiting for the next opportunity to jump. Just because you can't see it doesn't mean it isn't there.

In Summary

Society would rather have us pretend everything is okay than have us express our emotions. All this does is lead to repression and depression. It's time we open up and start talking about mental health.

Next: Understanding your role in your mental health

Chapter 3

The Part You Play in Your Mental Health

You feel hopeless. You think this is your status quo, that you're committed to a life of misery.

You aren't. That's just what you tell yourself to make yourself feel better about not *getting* better. I told myself the same things. I told myself I was destined to live with my depression forever.

In truth, you have every chance to make your life better…but you choose not to.

You're afraid of what it means to not be depressed. Your self-image is buried in who you are as a mentally ill person. Depression is who you are, and you don't know who you would be without it.

My depression was my identity. It was everything I knew. I always thought I would have to find a way to live and deal with my depression.

It means challenging everything you know. But if it means there's something better on the other side, why wouldn't you want to go through with it?

The Biology of Mental Illness

There is a great debate over what causes mental illness. Nobody knows for sure what causes it, but there are a few things that may contribute:

- Genetics

- Loneliness

- Brain injury

- Life experiences

- Stressful situations

- Traumatic experiences

- Previous mental illness

- History of abuse or neglect

- An ongoing medical condition

     Use of alcohol/recreational drugs

A chemical imbalance has been a popular theory, but new research (Ucl. "Analysis: Depression Is Probably Not Caused by a Chemical Imbalance in the Brain – New Study." UCL News, July 21, 2022. https://www.ucl.ac.uk/news/2022/jul/analysis-depression-probably-not-caused-chemical-imbalance-brain-new-study) indicates depression may not be caused by a chemical imbalance.

Nobody comes out of the womb depressed or anxious, but genetics may predispose you to mental illness.

On average, 50 percent of mental disorders start by age 14 and 75 percent begin by age 24.

This makes sense if you consider what's normally going on during these life periods. Around age 14, people are going into puberty, which causes a slew of hormone changes.

By age 24, you've graduated college and are entering the workforce. You're "adulting" now, for the first time.

Both are ages where you experience more stress as you navigate life changes. One is as you're transitioning from kid to teenager, and the next is as you're evolving into an adult. Every season of my life had its peaks and valleys. The height of my depression typically happened in tumultuous years when I was going through significant life changes, whether it was my teenage or college years.

The History of Treatment

For a long time, there was no real treatment for mental disorders. You were simply labeled "crazy" and committed to a mental institution. It wasn't until the 1950s that psychiatric drugs first appeared as treatment. Medications like chlorpromazine and imipramine were introduced as treatment options.

The psychiatry and pharmaceutical industry developed the "chemical imbalance" marketing strategy to sell these drugs. Big Pharma benefitted by calling all things psychological "chemical imbalances." Big Pharma, short for pharmaceuticals, is the collective representation of pharmaceutical companies across the globe.

You may recognize some of these companies, like Johnson & Johnson, Pfizer, and Merck.

Luckily, these companies provided the solution to our mental illnesses: pills marketed as "chemical balancers."

The public came to believe these "chemical balancers" were necessary to treat chemical imbalances in the brain. It was in the 1950s that Big Pharma came up with the idea that depression was the result of a chemical imbalance in the brain, a theory that remains to this day. However, there is no scientific evidence supporting this theory.

Researchers do not know how people develop chemical imbalances in the first place. And if depression were solely caused by a chemical imbalance, then treatments that target neurotransmitters should work faster.

If I believed my brain was deficient in serotonin, I would be apt to believe that I had no control over my illness beyond taking a pill that raised my serotonin. People who have this belief may feel helpless, but this belief is not true. In fact…

You Can Do Something

The idea that mental illness is caused by a chemical imbalance suggests that it's not your fault you have a mental illness, that you can't control whether you or not you have a chemical imbalance.

This is a cop-out. It makes it sound like you're doomed to have mental illness and you have no responsibility for it. This is how having mental disorders can become an excuse as to why you can't do something about them.

The implication that you have a responsibility for your illness is offensive to some. Many people believe that all you can really do for yourself is take drugs for it and nothing else.

In actuality, you *do* have responsibility. You can't lie down and play dead. You can't pretend that your mental illness completely inhibits you, because it doesn't. I was prescribed antidepressants in college, but they weren't effective, because a chemical imbalance simply isn't the whole picture.

Over the years, I've gone on and off medication (with the help of a doctor) and tried different varieties. I'm currently taking a regimen that works for me, but I wish I didn't need them.

Resistance is Futile

Having depression isn't fun by any means. When you have a mental illness, it's like having a dark side of yourself. It's like half of you is driven by the real illness you have, and the other half is the real you, unable to escape.

You're constantly in a battle between these two selves. The problem is the dark side of your mental health doesn't want to be treated. It wants to live in the shadows and feed off your despair.

Your mental illness is a hedonistic bastard. It takes joy in taking you down. But it's still part of you.

It's your dark side, and it feeds on your joy. It feeds on the darkness. And the more you give into your illness, the more power you give your dark side.

In a way, you currently depend on your illness. You've attached a sense of your self-identity to this idea of mental illness, and the suggestion that it might not be real is a threat.

It's a threat to you, and it's a threat to your mental illness.

The harsh truth is that you don't want treatment. It's hard to get treatment when you don't want it or you're not ready for it. Your mental illness takes pleasure in your pity, and your pity is steeped in your self-worth.

Admitting that you could do something to change your circumstances threatens everything you know about yourself and your life. The thought of getting better feels worse than staying where you are.

I was unwilling to face myself. In 2020, I avoided therapy because I knew it would force me to face the ugly truth. I didn't want to change. I wanted to revel in my depression because I got a sick sense of pleasure from it.

Be An Active Participant

"Sometimes you climb out of bed in the morning and you think, I'm not going to make it, but you laugh inside—remembering all the times you've felt that way." —Charles Bukowski

You depend on your mental illness. It gives you a sense of self, and it's easier to play dead than to work.

It's easier to call it quits and shut the world out than to do the hard work of letting it in.

Life isn't easy. But that's what makes it beautiful. The pain you feel is what allows you to feel pleasure.

It's time you admit your part in your mental illness and do something about it. You don't have to feel depressed all the time. You're not helpless. Your sense of self isn't just the dark side of you—it's the light side, too.

And until you can admit your part in this, you will always be submitted to a life of torture.

When I had my psychotic break, I hit my final rock bottom. I was 27 and admitted to the mental hospital. When I was in recovery in the hospital, there was one recurring theme the doctors kept bringing up:

You have to be an active participant in your recovery.

I recognized the truth of that statement and was determined to be an active participant.

You can't just give up and pray it all gets better. If you want to get better, you have to take responsibility for yourself into your hands. If you want your life to be different, you have to choose to be different.

I've been depressed for over 15 years, and I hated every second of it. I hated it so much that I was determined to climb out of the hole I was thrown in. I spent a lot of time in introspection, asking myself the tough questions, like: What was I avoiding in life? What traumas did I need to resolve? What did I want for myself?

I spent time journaling, letting my thoughts and emotions run free. There were a lot of ups and downs, but eventually, I got there.

You're not destined for a life of mental illness. It doesn't have to be that way, but healing requires your recognition that you have a part to play in your sickness.

In Summary

There are many things that can cause mental illness. But regardless of the cause, you play a role in your treatment. You can either resist or do something about it. Choose to be an active participant.

You don't have to be depressed forever.

You don't have to live in fear.

Make the choice to change. You can do it.

Next: depression roots itself in your identity

Section 2

Awareness

Chapter 4

Self-Identity Rooted in Depression

Who are you?

That was the question posed to us by my college English teacher. She asked us to take a few minutes to write down our answers.

As I stared down at my paper, nothing came to mind. I was clueless and unhappy with the answers I came up with. So, I finally just wrote something down.

For whatever reason, my teacher selected me out of all of the students and asked me to share my response.

I glanced down at my paper, then loudly stated, "I am not a label."

She laughed. "Maggie's not playing my game."

She was right. My self-identity was more complicated than could fit on one page.

What is Self-Identity?

Your self-identity is how you refer to yourself. It's the answer to the question "who are you?"

When I said, "I am not a label," I was proud. I wasn't confining myself to labels or boxes because I believe a human can't be put in a box. The human spirit is wild and free and can't be nailed down.

But that doesn't stop self-identity from being a thing. You still need a way to understand yourself. So, you decide on your self-identity.

Self-identity is the awareness and identification of oneself. It's all the labels you give yourself. It's how you understand yourself.

It's formed by internalizing values from your surroundings. Often, you will internalize the values you learned from your parents.

A runner, friend, sister, and daughter. All those labels apply to me, but no single one defines me.

Identity Crisis And Threats to Your Self-Identity

It's necessary to have a strong sense of self. When you don't, you're at risk for constant identity crises. I've been through my fair share of them, and they aren't fun. Once, in college, I took an existentialism course. I was fascinated by the subject, but it wasn't for me. It caused me daily existential crises, so I ended up dropping the class.

There will be many times throughout your life when your self-identity comes into question. You will always question your identity, as it is ever-evolving. You choose your value.

However, there are a few things in particular that may incite a crisis. Any of the following may provoke an identity crisis:

- Moving

- Job change

- Traumatic event

- Loss of a loved one

- Mental health issues

- Physical health issues

- Change in relationship(s)

It's typically in times of change where stress weighs on your identity. Stress degrades your resources and targets you. It comes for your physical energy, wearing you down to the bone, before it takes over your mental capacity.

When you're going through an identity crisis, it can be rough. You may not even know you're in one, so here are some signs you may be experiencing an identity crisis:

- You feel you have no purpose

- You have low self-esteem

- You are feeling lost/aimless

- You are emotionally scattered

- You are questioning your values

- You have increased insecurity, anxiety, or depression

The feeling of losing your identity can be scary. It's hard when you don't know who you are and you're constantly questioning yourself.

If you don't know who you are, it may lead to depression, and in another "fun" feedback loop, having depression may lead to a lost sense of self, and so on. When I was in college, I didn't know who I was most days. I couldn't tell you what I wanted. I don't know about you, but this isn't my idea of fun.

The big problem with this is when you start to identify with negative emotions and thoughts. This is a problem for those with mental illness. Instead of identifying as "artist" or "good friend," you start to identify as "depressed" or "anxious," and suddenly that's who you become. It's very difficult to get out of that pit.

Entrenched in Depression

Your depression is a part of you, one of the labels you attach to yourself. But when you attach this to yourself, you're putting your self-identity in danger.

You become "someone who is depressed." "Depression" becomes your identity, and it can drown out your other labels until it's the only "part of you" that remains.

But mental states can change. The problem with identifying *as* a mental state, *as* a negative emotion like depression, you risk discomfort any time you're not depressed.

If you feel joy, you think to yourself, "this isn't right—I'm supposed to be depressed. I'm a depressed person." You are unable to appreciate the fact that emotions are fleeting. You are unable to feel comfortable with who you are as you begin to heal.

Your mental illness is part of your identity right now, for better or worse. It's been around so long that you're used to it being there. You get so used to certain symptoms, limitations, and failures associated with your illness that you believe they comprise who you are.

Despite depression being a part of your identity, it shouldn't define who you are. Like how those labels of "daughter" and "runner" didn't completely define me, your depression doesn't completely define you. Depression is not who you are.

People are more than the labels society tries to box them into.

Your Emotions Are Lying to You

More often than not, your emotions are not even accurate. It's easy to assume that you process your emotions in a logical way. Something makes you mad, so you feel mad. Something makes you happy, so you feel happy.

Let's take a look at the famous "Love Bridge" study. In the study, 85 men walked across an unsteady, shaky bridge 200 feet up above shallow waters. After they stepped off the bridge, they were approached by an attractive woman who offered her name and phone number for them to call.

The men were compared to a second group, who walked across a stable bridge and were again approached by an attractive woman who offered her name and phone number.

The men on the unstable bridge were significantly more likely to call the woman than the men on the stable bridge. So, what happened here?

On the unstable bridge, the men were placed in a position of fear. Their body went into a state of arousal where all of their senses were heightened.

The men on the stable bridge had lower rates of fear and arousal.

When the men on the unstable bridge walked off and were approached by the woman, they accidentally misattribute their state of arousal to sexual attraction. The men didn't even think of the fact that they just stepped off a terrifying bridge. Nobody realized their emotional arousal had *nothing* to do with the woman.

This phenomenon is known as the misattribution of arousal. It means people make mistakes determining where their arousal comes from.

This also applies to depression. People misattribute their lack of purpose and sadness to their flaws or their mistakes, instead of recognizing it as depression.

Diversify Your Identity

"When you have money, it's always smart to diversify your investments. That way if one of them goes south, you don't lose everything. It's also smart to diversify your identity, to invest your self-esteem and what you care about into a variety of different areas—business, social life, relationships, philanthropy, athletics—so

> *that when one goes south, you're not com-*
> *pletely screwed over and emotionally*
> *wrecked."—Mark Manson*

If you simply label yourself as a "depressed person," you're always going to be depressed because you didn't give yourself the opportunity to be anything but.

The fix to that is to diversify your identity. In the same way you don't put all your eggs in one basket, you don't want to put your whole identity into one thing.

You are made up of so much more than just depression. Recognize that, and diversify. Understand that just because you feel depressed does not mean depression is a part of you.

I am made up of all the things I love and that love me. I'm made of my love for music, my love for my family, and my love for travel, among many others.

Reframing Your Mindset

Words matter. As a writer, this is something I know very well. Writing is an art. Every word is like a brush stroke, and you're the painter. You have to paint this beautiful picture and write elegant prose.

The point is, your words matter. The things you tell yourself matter because those are the things you end up repeating in times of depression.

Everything you say to yourself makes a difference. It's a self-fulfilling prophecy. What you believe determines your thoughts and actions. You think and behave in a way that will ultimately confirm your beliefs.

If you change what you say to yourself, you can change your beliefs. Stop saying you hate yourself, and you might stop hating yourself. Point out all the things you love about yourself. Affirm those things every day. Allow yourself to feel positive things.

In Summary

You can take the reins and diversify your identity. Don't let yourself be pigeonholed, especially not by your mental illness. You are so much more than whatever that part of you is.

You get to define who you are, nobody else.

Remember that your identity is multifaceted. You are more than the labels prescribed by yourself or society. Don't lose yourself to stress. Diversify your identity.

Next: how you self-sabotage

Chapter 5

Self-sabotage

In the past, I've engaged in various destructive behaviors.

I binge-watched TV while I binge-ate, only to cry myself to sleep. I self-isolated and let my depression take hold of me. I stop taking care of myself and let life slip by, apathetic to reality.

These are my self-destructive behaviors.

It was and is a sickness.

I went through major life changes in the past couple of years. My mom and I have a running joke about everything that's gone wrong. I call it "The Shit List" and I've been adding to it since 2013, when I first took a semester off college.

Within the past 10 years, my aunt and grandpa died. I watched my dad and dog die. I had fainting spells that landed me in the hospital. Then, I had a psychotic break that landed me in the mental hospital. It's been an eventful few years, but I've come out on the other side of it as a stronger person.

As that person, I don't want to slip back into old behaviors just because they're comfortable.

Unfortunately, sometimes life gets the best of us.

It's easy to fall back into familiar patterns. With the death of my family members, I struggled to cope. I fell back into bad habits.

You have to be self-aware enough to recognize them, and strong enough to grow beyond them.

Conscious and Unconscious Sabotage

Self-sabotage can happen both consciously and unconsciously. Consciously, you may decide to not exercise even when you are committed to a daily exercise regime.

Unconsciously, you may be repeating early conditioning and learned behaviors.

For me, there were times when I consciously knew I should go for a run. I knew it would make me feel better. But unconsciously, I hated myself and wanted to self-destruct. Guess who didn't go on a run?

When your identity is connected to your mental disorder, there's a part of you that gets used to it being around. As such, you may subconsciously self-sabotage to keep that part of your identity intact.

Your identity doesn't like being threatened. Often, when it is threatened you turn to self-sabotaging behaviors to preserve it, even though you may not be consciously aware of it.

Other common reasons for self-sabotaging include:

- Low self-worth

- Instant gratification

- You saw it modeled in your family

- Fear of rejection/failure

- Familiar (despite being harmful) patterns

All this can happen without you realizing it. Just like with depression, if no one talks about it, it's become harder and harder to know when it's happening to you.

Recognizing Self-Sabotage

Self-sabotaging behaviors aren't always recognizable.

You may be self-sabotaging if you participate in any of the following:

1. You avoid responsibility.

You use procrastination as a way to avoid taking responsibility for your actions. It allows you to blame your circumstances on external factors.

Stop blaming other people and circumstances and take personal accountability for your life. When you can do this, you empower yourself to make the right choices.

When you make a mistake, own it. Apologize for it and make a promise to yourself to do better.

2. You self-medicate.

You turn to drugs and alcohol to ease the pain in your chest. You use food to fill up the numbness inside of you. For me, my binge-eating made me feel less hollow.

If self-medication is a problem for you, reach out to a support group. There are great resources like NAMI that can get you the help you need.

Support groups can help give you resources like how to cope with addiction and learn more about what drives your behavior. Otherwise you'll be dealing with the symptoms and never the cause.

3. You ignore your physical health

You haven't exercised in months and you can't remember the last time you ate a vegetable. Maybe it was when you had that pizza last week. I have a real problem where I neglect my health by ignoring exercise and binge-eating instead.

Try to build a routine slowly. Plan to incorporate five minutes of movement into your day and add greens to one meal a day.

Today, you could eat one salad or walk to the end of the block. Make small commitments to improve your health.

4. You don't do anything.

You sit there paralyzed, doing nothing. You decide to watch Netflix instead of getting anything done. For a solid year, I did nothing in my life except watch YouTube and Netflix. I was unaware of how much I was sabotaging myself.

Bite off little bits at a time. Complete the smallest task on your list, like calling someone, or spending five minutes working on your essay.

What I like to do is keep a jar of tasks I like to do. When I'm feeling stuck, I'll pick one and do that one task.

5. You want to be liked.

All you want to do is be liked. You want to make everyone happy, so you bend over backward and ignore your own happiness. I understand wanting to make people happy. I value my peace over everything, so I people please to keep the peace.

However, to find true peace, you must spend less time worrying about others and more time focusing on yourself. Allow yourself time for self-care every day and stick to it.

Take a few minutes today and journal your thoughts and feelings. It will help you gain clarity.

6. You only look for the bad things in life

Negativity is like a soul-crushing vortex. It sucks away anything good in your life and replaces it with darkness. It serves no purpose.

Start looking for the good things in life. Reaffirm positive things that happen. If it helps, try mantras or affirmations.

Repeat things to yourself like, "I can do anything," or, "There is nothing that can stop me."

7. You criticize yourself.

You make self-deprecating jokes and comments for a laugh, hiding behind the truth. You put yourself down and beat yourself up.

Stop playing the blame game. You're not to blame, but you are responsible for your actions. Instead of criticizing, try problem-solving.

Ask yourself, "Why?" Are you uncomfortable? Poor self-esteem? Get clear about why you are doing it and do something about it.

The Hard Road of Awareness

"Sometimes we self-sabotage just when things seem to be going smoothly. Perhaps this is a way to express our fear about whether it is okay for us to have a better life. We are bound to feel anxious as we leave behind old notions of our unworthiness. The challenge is not to be fearless, but to develop strategies of acknowledging our fears and finding out how we can allay them." — Maureen Brady

Self-sabotage is an easy path to take. From procrastination to self-criticism, we know all the tricks in the book. Your self-sabotaging patterns are ingrained in you. They are like defense mechanisms, something to protect you from everything going wrong. But eventually, they do more harm than good.

There is a mourning process as you start to tackle your mental health. You've become so used to having depression that it feels foreign to not have it. That's why you start to self-sabotage. It keeps you from having to mourn that loss of identity.

Self-sabotaging won't get you anywhere in the long term, though. You have to push past it to get to the other side.

The most important part of defeating self-destructive behavior is becoming aware of it. Once you become aware you can work on other aspects, such as:

- Becoming more assertive

- A stronger sense of autonomy

- Not being afraid of conflict

- Knowing how to set boundaries

- Expressing your feelings

- Taking initiative

- Liking yourself as you are

These are not easy steps to accomplish, but once you've identified the action you need to take, you can begin working toward a solution. You're not indebted to a life of misery or self-sabotage. You can beat it.

When I become aware of my bad habits, like eating poorly, I can course correct and make better decisions the next time around.

In Summary

You may not be aware of all the ways you self-sabotage, but you can become aware. Become aware of your patterns. Pay attention to how you may sabotage, both consciously and unconsciously.

Next: you don't have to hit rock bottom

Hitting Rock Bottom

It took a long time for me to hit rock bottom, but when I did, I went out with a bang. I spent three long days getting intermittent sleep and coming up with ideas I thought would change the world.

None of my ideas made any sense though. As the days progressed, my brain deteriorated until one night, my brain snapped. I had a psychotic break. After years of trauma boiling up inside me, I finally broke. I guess you can only hold so much trauma before you break.

When this happened, I was committed to a mental hospital.

Hitting rock bottom was a rough experience, especially because I involved other people in it. It didn't just affect me; it affected my mom and sister, too.

When someone you love hits rock bottom, you experience some of it with them. My family felt helpless and experienced severe distress, mirroring many of my own feelings.

Some may believe that hitting rock bottom is the only way to recover. Only once you've hit your lowest point, they believe, are you able to turn around and climb out of the grave you dug for yourself.

But I didn't have to hit rock bottom to get help, and neither do you. You can choose to make a turning point on your own. You don't have to wait for rock bottom to happen before you decide you need help. If you do hit rock bottom, though, this advice may help you.

Wanting Help

I wanted to get better and recover from my depression but was determined to do it on my own. Since I didn't like feeling like I wasn't in control, I was determined to get control back.

But sometimes you're hit with revelations when you least expect it. I was journaling one day when it hit me: "You're not showing up for yourself." Maybe you're feeling a similar revelation while reading this book. Maybe something you read here struck a chord with you and you've decided to make it a turning point.

You can create your own turning points. I did. I had multiple turning points—after most of them, I would get better, only to fall off and allow my depression to progress again.

At the end of my sophomore year in college I skipped classes and stopped doing the assignments. I lay under my bed sheets when I was supposed to be in class. My depression was so bad I had to take a semester off.

I had no accountability and no purpose. I wanted to get better but didn't have any driving forces in my life.

Essentially, I never felt like my depression was bad enough. I would convince myself I didn't have depression at all. But I was only setting myself up to fail.

Depression is sneaky that way. It convinces you it doesn't exist, only to reappear at the worst times. Eventually, my attempts to regain control by myself failed, and I ended up in the hospital. It was only when I had nowhere else to go that I finally found external help.

The Silver Lining

"Hitting rock bottom doesn't mean that you have to stay there." —Michelle Parsons

Rock bottom is never where you want to go, but sometimes you need to hit your emotional threshold and lose everything before you can recover. You're going to be faced with dark, difficult decisions. Breaking down serves as a wake-up call. Even during such a difficult time, I tried to find the bright side of hitting rock bottom and surviving. These bright sides include:

1. You reinvent yourself

Hitting rock bottom allows you to reassess your life and what you're doing with it. It's a chance to reassess your relationships, values, and goals. And if it so suits you, you're granted the chance to change them.

It tested my relationships with my mom and sister, and it also deepened them.

Getting through those difficult times is like getting a second lease on life. It could be the best thing to ever happen to you because it makes you open your eyes and realize what you've been missing.

2. You gain empathy

When you hit rock bottom, you experience dozens of different emotions. You feel overcome with sadness and can't get up from it. However, from the ground, you see things differently.

You realize what true pain is and you see the others around you who are also hurting. Some of the other in-patients had moving, tragic stories.

Lisa was in the hospital for her depression. Before she was admitted, her mom had a severe stroke, and when Lisa was in the hospital, her dad committed suicide.

Becky was in the hospital for drug abuse following the death of her 22-year-old son, who died of an overdose.

When you're at rock bottom, you're mainly focused on yourself and your own pain, as you should be. But as you get better and get back on your feet, you gain perspective.

You know how bad it was, so you realize just how deeply people can go down through the hole. You start to recognize that other people are coping with similar emotions and you can identify with them. This can help both of you heal.

3. You become resilient

Resilience grows from adversity. It can only grow when you're faced with difficult tests of being and willpower. Like a phoenix, you rise from the ashes more powerful than before. You become brave, wise, and fearless.

You've overcome the most difficult obstacle life could throw at you, and you came out on the other side. This boosts your confidence and willpower to be able to say you can overcome anything.

4. You step outside your comfort zone

You've now overcome one of the worst things you will ever face in your life. Doesn't that give you a small sense of victory? It makes you feel like you can accomplish anything. It gives you the strength and courage to put yourself out there.

You have a new lease on life, and it's giving you chances to go after what you want. What's something you've always wanted to do but were always too scared to try? Have you started that business? Written that book? Taken that pole dancing class?

I always put off writing a book because I was nervous about the reaction it would get. But I moved through my fears, and here I am.

It'll be scary getting out of your comfort zone, but you've faced worse. It will be scary, but it will be worth it.

5. You become grateful

The absolute worst has happened to you, and you're still standing. It's a miracle. And you find that you start to appreciate the little things in life. You become thankful you can see. You become thankful flowers exist. You become thankful for morning coffee with your mom. You see life lessons as gifts given to you.

6. You gain humility

You realize that life isn't black and white and that you don't know everything. In fact, you realize that there's so much more to life that you don't yet know, and this gives you humility.

When you realize what other people are going through, your problems don't seem as bad. Having a dead dad and psychotic break was pretty bad, but so was having your parent commit suicide. You are not alone in your pain, even if it seems that way.

7. You take responsibility

Perhaps for the first time, you're starting to accept full responsibility for your actions. You realize blaming is futile and complaining is dumb. Making excuses no longer suits you and your needs.

You realize that it's you who's responsible for all the good and bad in your life, and it's your responsibility to climb out of the hole.

What to Do When You Hit Rock Bottom

Now that you're at rock bottom, you're looking up and wondering where the ladder is. If you're ready to start climbing, then let's go! Here's what you need to do:

1. Believe in yourself

It's easier said than done, but you should learn how to believe in yourself. If there's one person in your life that has your back, it should be yourself. You can't count on anyone else to believe in you, but you can believe in yourself. I've put up sticky notes on my mirror to remind me of this.

Don't let anyone else put you down or discourage you. Keep moving forward and never back down.

2. Feel your pain

You have to be able to feel your emotions, even the worst of them. Feel your sadness and pain. Don't hold it in. When you repress your emotions, you're setting yourself up for a breakdown. You may feel like going down an easy street, but ultimately, feeling your emotions is better for you.

Repressing my feelings didn't get me anywhere. Only once I allowed myself to feel the pain from my dad's death was I able to move on.

Pain is a difficult emotion. Nobody likes to be in pain, but the pain is necessary for life. You may not *want* to experience pain, but it's a cornerstone for human development.

Without pain, there would be no contrast to pleasure. You need pain if you want pleasure.

3. Practice self-compassion

Self-compassion doesn't always come naturally, but you can work to improve it. Pay attention to your thought patterns and when you put yourself down. When you recognize yourself doing so, choose to stop and challenge the thought.

Be kind to yourself. It's a learning curve, but you can do it. Start to become aware and shift your language to something more positive. Affirmations work well for this. One of my favorite affirmations is one I came up with: "My power is too great to be contained."

4. Be responsible for yourself

It's the last thing you want to hear, but you need to take responsibility for your actions, both the good and the bad. Having a sense of responsibility will give you back control over your life and make you feel happier.

When you take responsibility, you're saying, "I'm responsible for my life." It empowers you to realize you can take the actions that will change your life.

My life has gotten significantly better since doing this. By taking responsibility, my actions have more weight and I'm more mindful of what I do.

5. Find your home

Home isn't always a physical place. Sometimes it's a thing, feeling, or person. Home is somewhere you feel safe and comfortable.

What does home feel like to you? For me, music is my home. It's something I can turn to whenever and wherever I am, and it makes me feel comfortable and safe.

6. Spend time in nature

Spending time in nature can be wonderful for your recovery. Connecting with your roots and the Earth brings you back to yourself.

One of my favorite things to do is spend time in the water. It's completely freeing and relaxing.

7. Spend time with positive people

As you find yourself recovering, share it with your loved ones. It's important to surround yourself with others who are positive, helpful, and supportive of you.

Surrounding yourself with a positive network of people will help you get back on your feet faster.

8. Create a recovery plan and seek professional help

Tackling your struggles is not easy. Once you accept it, it gets easier. Now you can make sense of what's happened and create an action plan to go forward.

Look for advice from people you trust. Talk to your friends, families, or professional therapists. Set yourself some long- and short-term goals that you can look forward to.

Don't put too much pressure on yourself. Take your time. Recovery is a slow process.

Eventually, baby steps will get you where you need to go.

In Summary

Hitting rock bottom isn't necessary for your recovery. You can create your own turning points and avoid it. But, in the case you do hit rock bottom, there are things you can do to take advantage of it.

Next: the importance of reaching out for support

Section 3

Seeking Treatment

Chapter 7

Reaching Out for Support

Long before I was committed to the mental hospital, I was living in West Hollywood. At the time, I was 25. It was a horrible experience. The apartment was infested with bugs and I was constantly anxious. To top it off, I was at the height of my depression.

So there I was, lying on the sofa bed, sobbing. The pain was extreme and I knew I didn't want to keep feeling that way.

I opened a voice memo on my phone and started recording. I bawled my eyes out, only managing to get a few words out in between.

"I need help."

I titled it "Get help." I went to bed early that night and slept in. The next morning, I was functioning. I opened my phone and saw the voice recording. I remembered making it, but was struck by the title.

I recalled feeling awful, and I knew I didn't ever want to feel that way again. It was time.

I got on my computer and researched, looking for local mental health support. Eventually, I found the LGBT+ center and saw they offered therapy. I made an initial appointment. Then, I waited.

The good news is, outside forces tend to make me accountable. So, I knew setting up the appointment would make me get out of the house and go.

At my doctor's appointment, they prescribed me antidepressants and Vitamin D. This time, I was on Lexapro and it was much more effective than my last medication, Celexa.

Becoming Aware

The hardest part of having a mental illness is recognizing it's a real problem, that it's not all just in your head.

You've convinced yourself for so long that it isn't a problem. You've convinced yourself this is something you have to live with. You've convinced yourself there is no help.

There *is* help out there. But you have to recognize the problem first.

That night in LA, I recognized I had a real problem. I spent most of my nights crying, in unbearable pain. It got to the point where I realized that this pattern was impeding me and my life. I became aware of the giant elephant in the room: my thoughts.

Reaching Out for Help

You've now moved on to a vital part of recovery. Once you've decided to get help, you can make inroads toward changing your life.

You've taken the step of recognizing the problem. You're aware of it. Now, you need to make others aware of it. What does that look like?

Tell your friends and family what you're going through. Sit down with them and explain what's going on. Tell them that you're suffering and that you're seeking support.

It's best to address your thoughts in a professional setting, so the next part is seeing a therapist.

Talk therapy is powerful. By sitting down with a professional, in a safe setting, you can start to unravel your deepest, darkest secrets.

I've been to therapy off and on through the years, meeting an array of different therapists. All of them took different approaches, but not all were successful.

One therapist spent our entire session validating my struggles and stroking my ego. It was not helpful and I did not return to them. Another therapist taught me Cognitive Behavioral Therapy (CBT) techniques to help work through my problems. This proved to be more beneficial, so I continued to see her.

Setting Up a Therapy Appointment

You'll want to do some research on therapists in your area. Look for a therapist that specializes in your illness. Filter through if you want a young or old therapist, a female or male therapist.

Chances are, there are plenty of therapists in your area, but picking the right one is a process. You might not find the right fit on the first go.

Explore how they work through problems. Some therapists may use cognitive behavioral therapy (CBT) or something else. Understanding their methods is going to be important in how you start to heal.

You want a therapist that you're comfortable talking to.

When looking for a good fit, consider these traits. A good therapist will:

- Validate your problems

- Listen to you

- Be a strong communicator

- Take time to educate themselves

- Earn your trust

- Challenge you

- Offer a range of solutions

- Not rush your treatment

- Give you the tools to do the work

They won't be your best friend. They're not intended to be.

Be careful with this though. If you find yourself hopping around from therapist to therapist, it's not the therapist that has a problem. It's you. You're resisting. You're avoiding.

When I first started going to therapy at the beginning of 2020, I kept bouncing around from therapist to therapist. I would say I didn't like them and they didn't understand me.

The truth was, I didn't give each therapist an honest chance. They would ask me questions I was unwilling to answer and give me work I was unprepared to do.

You can't do the work unless you are ready to do the work. You might still need time before you're ready, and that's okay.

Be honest with yourself. Do you want the treatment? Are you ready to do the work?

Being in therapy will put you in uncomfortable positions, and you have to be ready to deal with that. You're going to have to address uncomfortable thoughts and bring up traumatic events.

You might not be ready to deal with it yet. It's that resistance talking again. You can push through it. You can still go to therapy and talk about surface-level problems while you're establishing trust and a relationship with your therapist.

Eventually, you will feel more comfortable and ready to dive deep.

As you start going to therapy, hopefully, you will start to see results. Talk therapy is a strong treatment for depression.

After my experience in the mental hospital, I saw a therapist at my doctor's recommendation. This time, everything fell into place. It was a good match and I was finally in a place where I could resolve my issues.

Getting Into Psychiatry

You think that going on medication will solve all of your problems. It will not. Medication is a bandage, not a solution.

Medication is designed to level the bar to help you do things. It does not make you do things. That part is on you. If you want to get into psychiatry, it's going to be like therapy, where you need to be ready to do the work.

I see a psychiatrist in conjunction with a therapist. My psychiatrist manages my medications and it helps me stay stable and strong. But ultimately, as my therapist said, I'm the one who's doing all the work.

The Problem with Medication

Often, medication isn't effective. You have to consider the side effects and risks before taking them.

You won't get the right regimen right away. It takes time for antidepressants to kick in.

It took me three or four months before my medication started doing its job. And it took a whole lot of trial and error to get there. Often, I would try anxiety medication that would only make me more anxious.

When I went on Zoloft, it gave me rashes and night shakes. Zyprexa stopped my periods. I also had trouble sleeping.

I was tired all the time. I didn't get my energy back for months. But when the right medicine finally kicked in, I felt stable and happy.

But pills are not the answer to your problem; they're only part of it.

Big pharmaceutical companies want you to believe otherwise, because it's good for their bottom line.

The truth is, although antidepressants are used to enhance serotonin in the brain, there is evidence that the benefits may be due to the placebo effect. (I;, Kirsch. "Antidepressants and the Placebo Effect." Zeitschrift fur Psychologie. U.S. National Library of Medicine. Accessed October 9, 2022. https://pubmed.ncbi.nlm.nih.gov/25279271/) Ultimately, my greatest success came from what I did for myself, rather than the drugs I took.

In Summary

Reaching out for help is an important step in your recovery. Nobody can do it alone. You can do it with the help of your friends, family, and licensed therapist. You may even feel it's necessary to try medication; just keep in mind that medication is only part of the solution.

Next: what it means to do the work

Chapter 8

Do the Inner Work

Now that you know about your identity and how it works to sabotage itself, you're on your way.

You've admitted you have a problem and you're seeking help. Now, it's time to do the hard work. This is the fun part.

You've started going to therapy, you're talking about your problems. You're working your way toward healing and being free. Of course, that means you'll be dealing with pain.

Through The Pain

"People go through so much pain trying to avoid pain." —Neil Strauss

Going through pain teaches you adversity. Going through adversity is what makes you stronger. You will never get strong in life if you don't go through the pain of adversity. Nothing can go your way all the time.

There will be times when the going gets rough, and it puts you to the test. For a few years, it was one hardship after another on me and my family. We went through a period where everybody was dying and our appliances kept breaking.

The result of hardship is that it teaches you empathy and humility. When you experience pain, you realize the humanity in it. You recognize pain as bad and can empathize with those who share it.

Pain teaches you humility because it shows you you're not invincible. Pain shows you that you can be knocked down a peg or two. Sometimes ending up in the dirt forces you to take a realistic look at yourself.

From the ground, you either learn humility or to be a tool. Hopefully, you learn humility. You learn to be a tool if you have expectations about how life should be easy and you shouldn't have to go through hardships. Thinking this way will only lead you to more pain down the road. It's best if you learn humility now.

Ultimately, pain teaches you about yourself. You learn what you're made of and what your limits are. Pain tests your character. Once you're through it, you can do what you were incapable of doing before.

Called into Action

At this point, hopefully, you've addressed your part in your mental illness. You recognize where your problem is.

You've stopped blaming other people and other things for your problems. There's no longer anyone to blame but yourself.

It's not your parents' fault. It's not your teachers' fault. It's not society's fault. You are responsible for your own actions and beliefs.

Your initial reaction to this information may be reactive.

You may put up your defenses or play opossum.

You're taking on the personal responsibility to heal your wounds and recover. We've been talking about the work, but now you're going to be doing the real work.

You may be wondering what that looks like. There are a few different forms. Everybody is going to be different. Everyone goes through the same process to achieve similar results, but everybody's journey is different.

My inner work took a lot of self-reflection and journaling. I had to sit with myself and feel uncomfortable emotions, like jealousy, anger, and grief. And slowly, I worked through it. I did the homework my therapists gave me and filled out sheets to help me uncover my unconscious patterns.

Instead of feeling called out for your transgressions, you feel called in to do the work. You're ready.

Inner work is shaping your emotions, beliefs, and attitudes to create a healthier and happier version of yourself. It's about adjusting and correcting your mindset so that it helps you better facilitate your goals.

Inner work brings you light, compassion, and awareness to the conscious, subconscious, and unconscious realms of your being.

It's about diving inward: speaking to yourself, being in connection and dialogue with yourself, seeing yourself, knowing yourself, and loving yourself.

Shadow Work

During his career, Swiss psychologist Carl Jung popularized shadow work. Shadow work is defined as working with your unconscious mind to uncover the parts of yourself that you repress and hide. Your shadow is the dark, emotional side of your psyche.

Your shadow depends on what you subconsciously reject within yourself. It typically comes out through negative self-talk. These rejected parts of ourselves are often the result of childhood trauma.

Anyone can do shadow work on their own, but if you have deeper trauma you may consider seeking a licensed therapist for treatment.

Ultimately, shadow work is about developing self-awareness, self-acceptance, and compassion.

My shadow was interesting to deal with. She was filled with all my insecurities and self-hatred. I had to confront hard truths, like the fact I didn't trust or love myself.

By accepting your shadow self, you can start to see how your thoughts and emotions influence your behavior. When you're aware of this, you can take control and empower yourself to live life more deliberately and consciously. You can start to show up as your authentic self.

How to Do It

1. Decide if you'll do the shadow work on your own or seek help

It can be helpful to have someone guide you through the process. A professional can also spot patterns you may not be aware of.

2. Practice spotting your inner shadow

You can start by spotting your habits, whether good or bad. Pay attention to your triggers that remind you of your past trauma.

I spent some time addressing my anger and would make note of what happened every time it flared up. Turns out, it was the result of not making time for myself.

3. Think back to your childhood

Explore the parts of your childhood which made you feel less than. Many children are told to "get over" their anger and sadness and, as a result, learn to repress them.

In conjunction with working with your shadow, it's excellent to get back in touch with your inner child and what they liked and wanted. My inner child was always creative and expressed herself through art, so I began to do the same.

4. Avoid shaming your shadow

Your shadow is a part of you. Extend compassion to the shadow side of yourself by practicing loving words of affirmation.

5. Meditate to observe your triggers

Once you notice the triggers that cause emotional reactions in you, you can meditate on them. Step back and observe what's happening, without judgment.

6. Keep a shadow journal

Keep a journal where you can let out all parts, good and bad, of yourself. It's important to listen to your shadow self. Don't censor yourself.

7. Express your inner shadow artistically

Art is a powerful tool to express yourself. It can be a good alternative if journaling isn't for you. Use whatever medium you like and allow yourself to feel all the emotions.

Music and writing are powerful tools for me. They allow me to express and process my emotions.

8. Start an inner dialogue

This may seem strange at first, but you can have a conversation with your shadow. Drop into an empty space and ask it a question. Remember, no judgment.

If you follow these steps, these are some of the many benefits you can gain from doing shadow work:

1. More confidence and self-esteem

2. Improved creativity

3. Better relationships with others

4. Self-acceptance

5. Discovered hidden talents

6. Improved overall wellness

7. Increased compassion toward others

8. Better clarity

Trauma-Focused Therapy

Trauma-Focused Therapy is a therapy approach that emphasizes how traumatic experiences impact a person's wellbeing.

The purpose of trauma-focused therapy is to offer skills and strategies to help you better understand your traumatic experiences. The end goal is to enable yourself to create a healthier meaning of the experience.

SAMHSA's Definition of a Trauma-Focused Therapy

"A program, organization, or system that is trauma-informed:

1. *Realizes* the widespread impact of trauma and understands potential paths for recovery;

2. *Recognizes* the signs and symptoms of trauma in clients, families, staff, and others involved with the system;

3. *Responds* by fully integrating knowledge about trauma into policies, procedures, and practices; and

4. Seeks to actively resist *re-traumatization*."

Your Inner Child

The concept of an inner child is also traced back to psychiatrist Carl Jung. Part of his shadow work included 8 archetypes, one of which represented the child inside you. This inner child is linked to your past experiences and memories, along with your hope for the future.

People tend to be protective over their childhood experiences, but you have a unique opportunity to heal yourself and consciously make different decisions than your parents.

This process is called reparenting. I started going through the process of reparenting right before my psychotic break. I had a few insights about my family structure, and how I needed validation from them. But unfortunately, it was cut short.

Reparenting is the act of giving yourself what you didn't receive as a child.

There are 4 pillars to reparenting, including:

- Discipline
- Joy
- Emotional regulation
- Self-care

Reparenting can be overwhelming, but it's a process. You won't be able to change it all overnight. It will take time, otherwise, you risk falling back into old patterns. Try not to do too much at once.

To begin the process of reparenting, first, breathe.

Second, keep one small promise to yourself every day. This step you pick should be small. Make it so small that it seems insignificant.

If you make big promises, you're more likely to break them. The point of small promises is that it's easy to keep them. For example, you decide to meditate for two minutes, walk to the end of the block and back, or journal each day. Do not choose anything that takes more than 10 minutes to complete. By keeping these promises, you build the trust within yourself that you need to facilitate future healing.

Don't share that you're doing this with your parents, as it can be hurtful to them. However, tell someone you trust that you're going through this process. Having support will be helpful.

As an adult, you have the opportunity to give yourself what you didn't receive as a child. Ask yourself, "What can I give myself right now?" You may not come up with an answer immediately, but keep asking. It's a practice of connecting to your intuition. If you stay committed, you'll begin to get answers.

Last, celebrate when you show up for yourself. Reparenting is difficult work. It takes courage. Celebrate the progress you're making and acknowledge the work you're doing.

In Summary

You can try one, or all, of the different methods described here of doing the work. Doing the inner work is where your healing takes place. You can work through your inner child, shadow work, and reparenting.

Next: making sure you implement the work

Implementing the Work

Before I went to the hospital, I was in the throes of climbing out of the depression hole. I found every self-improvement book I could get my hands on. I read them voraciously, tearing them apart and devouring the information.

Despite all my reading, I didn't feel any better. It's because I was too busy reading that I wasn't implementing it. When you don't implement the behaviors you desire, you're never going to change.

Real change requires taking action.

Reading Isn't Enough

Imagine: you're in high school reading your textbooks, but you don't take any notes or memorize the information. There's no chance you're going to do well on your test.

Reading is only as valuable as your ability to implement what you read. You can read all you want, but you won't get anywhere unless you do something with the information.

Don't just read this book and then put it back on the shelf to gather dust. Pick one thing out of the book that you can take action on and do it.

Taking Care of Yourself

When I lost my mind, it was scary as hell. I had zero control. Coming out of the hospital, I realized I have to pay close attention to how I'm treating myself.

I'm not going to lie, recovery is difficult. You're not going to be on top of your game every day, and that's okay. You're going to have some off days. What matters is that you get up the next morning and try again. Have your off days, but don't give into the temptation of giving up.

There are some things you can do that are proven to help:

- Meditation

Train your attention and awareness with meditation. By meditating, you can calm your mind and become mentally clear. Meditation helps you ease the tension and anxiety in your body.

You can choose to meditate on your own or use a guide. I use the app Headspace, but there are other options—such as Calm, Aura, or even just YouTube videos.

- Journaling

Journaling is great for your mental health. Writing down your thoughts, emotions, and experiences helps you work through your problems and improves the quality of your mental health.

It helps to manage stress and anxiety, and reduce depression. You can write anything that is comfortable for you. Having a journal can help you maintain the feeling of control in your life.

- Routine

Having a routine can help you manage stress. By setting routines, you will sleep better, enjoy better health, and be happier.

If you don't currently have a routine, start by creating one. Write down the things you do every day and make a schedule for yourself. If you already have a routine, consider tweaking it to better suit your needs.

- Sleep

Good sleep is essential to maintaining health. If you're not sleeping well, it can throw you off track.

Ways to get better sleep include setting (and keeping) a bedtime ritual, stretching before bed, and using less technology before bed.

- Diet

You hate to hear it, but it's true. Eating more food from the Earth helps your body. That means eating your fruits and vegetables. Eat lettuce, spinach, apple, bananas, and onions. Some of the world's oldest people are alive today due to eating plant-based diets.

You don't have to give up sweets completely, but learn to eat them in moderation and eat primarily plant-based. Your diet is a big part of getting and staying fit, both mentally and physically.

- Exercise

Make it a habit to move your body more often. While exercising is a great way to do it, you could incorporate more chores around the household. Anything that gets you moving contributes to a healthier lifestyle.

Experts say you should move vigorously for 30 minutes three times a week, but the biggest hurdle is getting a body moving. Try not to sit for too-long periods.

- Set realistic goals

Setting goals can help you stay on track. It gives you something to look forward to and work for.

Keeping that in mind, set *realistic* goals. If your goals are too outlandish, then you'll feel discouraged when you don't meet them—or when it takes a long time to meet them. You won't feel like you can possibly reach them, but this is not because you are a bad person—it's because you set the bar too high.

For example, say I wanted to incorporate exercise into your routine. If I'm starting out, setting a goal to work out for 1 hour every day might be a little farfetched. Right now, it's out of my reach. My goals should make sense. Instead of exercising for 1 hour, start with walking for 10 minutes.

-   Surround yourself with a support system

This part can be tough sometimes. It's easy to feel isolated and alone. You may feel like nobody understands what you're going through. You may feel like you don't have anyone to talk to.

You may not have a strong support system in real life. Your friends may all seem superficial and your family may be neglectful.

I'm lucky. My family was a great support system to lean on as I recovered. I strengthened my bonds with my mom and sister. As trying a time as it was, we came out on the other side stronger.

But some of the people I'm closest to I met online. You can try friend apps to meet new, like-minded people, or try searching forums on the internet.

The National Alliance for Mental Illness, better known as NAMI, has different support groups you can join based on your location. Just remember that no matter who you are, there's someone out there who wants to help you.

In Summary

You won't get anywhere without implementing the work. You can do all the homework you want, but it won't matter unless you take action. It's imperative that you learn to take care of yourself and build a trustworthy support system.

Next: the new mental health theory on the block

Chapter 10

How Polyvagal Theory is Revolutionizing Mental Health

There's a new theory on the scene that could revolutionize the way we treat mental health. And it's all dependent on your autonomic nervous system.

Your autonomic nervous system (ANS) is a system that involves tons of body parts and organs. The ANS regulates your heart rate, digestion, and respiratory rate. The ANS is the primary mechanism in charge of the fight-or-flight response. The vagus nerve links them all together.

The ANS is responsible for regulating all those automatic functions in your body that you don't control on your own.

Depending on your autonomic state, your body transforms and different systems are activated. This state is the filter through which you perceive the world.

What if we changed that filter? By understanding the polyvagal theory, you can understand your mental health in an entirely new way.

An Overview of Polyvagal Theory

The polyvagal theory is a new theory of how the nervous system works. The autonomic nervous system has previously been thought to have two states—the sympathetic and the parasympathetic.

The parasympathetic state is reserved for rest-and-digest functions and is where most people spend their time. You're in this state when you're at home washing the dishes or watching TV. The sympathetic state is responsible for fight-or-flight. You're engaged in the fight-or-flight state when you're running or playing sports.

The polyvagal theory introduces a third response option. Let's think of them like a traffic light.

Green is your safe space. That's where you're at rest and feel comfortable. It's the equivalent of the rest-and-digest function. This is your couch potato mode. In your safe space, your heart rate slows, saliva and digestion are activated, facial muscles are activated, and you increase vocal prosody and eye contact.

We'll call yellow your danger space. This is where you would find the fight-or-flight approach. In this state, your heart rate speeds up, pain tolerance goes up, and you flatten your facial tone. This is where you jump into action. It's normal for athletes to use this state, as it's part of the sport.

Red represents a third state: your freeze system. When your autonomic nervous system detects something life-threatening, it shuts down. Instead of doing anything or engaging, you freeze.

Healthy individuals can bounce between the green and yellow systems with ease, spending the least amount of time in the red state. This is good, as it's in the red zone that we experience trauma.

Trauma

The polyvagal theory says that prolonged exposure in the "red" zone allows us to better understand trauma. Typically when clinicians look at trauma, they look at it from the psychological side. They analyze trauma in terms of how it affects and makes you feel. But trauma isn't psychological. It's physiological.

Your instinct to freeze is completely involuntary and comes from hundreds of thousands of years of evolution.

In our modern world, we're faced with stressors on a daily basis. Most of the time, you can choose how to deal with them. But when you're taken by surprise, it's easy to freeze up.

Our ancestors didn't get the option to decide when something was dangerous. Their neuroception would jump in and provide an immediate response.

What would happen if we treated trauma as a physiological state? We would realize there is a greater threshold for people to feel "safe." We could use environmental and social cues to help people feel a sense of safety.

Your autonomic state is self-reinforcing. If you are safe, you sense safety, but if you are in danger you sense more danger. By knowing the polyvagal theory, you can use it to avoid exposure to the red zone and find your safe "green" zone.

You can also do exercises designed for the vagus nerve to help relieve stress.

How This Applies to Mental Health

Those with autism, depression, schizophrenia, anxiety, and borderline personality disorder all share the inability to feel safe. Some of this could be due to the ANS's response to prolonged trauma exposure.

This could also explain why I struggled to get out of depression on my own. If my depression were brought on by prolonged trauma exposure, I would be helpless to deal with it on my own. There would be no getting out of the depression until the trauma was resolved and I felt safe.

Feeling safe is crucial. Your "green" safe space is important for facilitating general health, releasing beneficial hormones, helping to learn, making life more enjoyable, and optimizing the human experience.

My green space looks like writing, listening to music, and spending time with my pets.

Nervous System Hacks To Find Your "Green" Space

If you're trying to calm and recenter yourself, you can try the following things to enter your safe space:

- Breathe slowly

- Speak with smiles, eye-contact, and a sing-songy voice

- Listen to mid-frequency music (such as Disney soundtracks)

- Work, learn, and live in environments that are "safe"

- Spend time around people you like and love

Feeling safe is *necessary* for living a good life and bonding with others. Once you have that, you'll find your safe space grows bigger and bigger every day.

In Summary

The polyvagal theory offers new insights into the world of mental health. It proposes three response states of your ANS and views trauma as a physiological response rather than psychological.

Next: how to find your version of happiness

Section 4

Maintenance

Chapter 11

Choosing Happiness

I used to think that I would never be happy. I used to think happiness was a myth. Then I thought that someday, through the grace of god, I would find happiness, and then I would be happy my whole life.

I was wrong.

Happiness isn't a destination. You don't reach happiness. But you can choose happiness every day.

Everybody wants to be happy. We look at happiness as the greatest achievement in life.

Unfortunately, I have bad news for you: happiness is not something you can achieve.

Depression always made me think that happiness was a goal. It made me think that everything in my life would be better if I could just be "happy." But after my recovery, I've come to realize the truth.

Happiness is an emotion. You feel happy the same way you feel tired, or you feel sad. Happy is an emotional state, and emotions are forever in flux.

Emotions are those fun things humans were equipped with that we never wanted, but needed.

You assume that you're working toward happiness. That you'll be happy someday.

You use statements like, "I'll be happy when I can pay the rent," "I'll be happy when I get a raise," "I'll be happy when…" And the list goes on.

This pervasive message in our culture about happiness and success says we have to be successful, and happiness is one more thing for us to acquire to achieve success.

"Happiness" has nothing to do with success.

Truth be told, being happy is way easier than you think it is.

When we talk about being happy, we mean something else. Instead of happiness, I think we want to be content.

Being content and being happy are similar, but the distinction is important. They're both emotions, but being content is like a level above happiness. "Content" doesn't fluctuate in the same way. Being content is more like a state of being that you can prolong.

If you are content, you are satisfied, which I think is ultimately what we're after. You want to feel satisfied in life. It fills you up inside.

If you're not satisfied, it feels like you have a hole in your chest or like something is missing. Being satisfied means you aren't chasing after this intangible source of meaning.

I feel content with my life, and I didn't for a long time. It took a psychotic break, ECT, and therapy before I was able to reframe my mindset. I stopped needing to chase happiness. Instead I was able to be present and *choose* happiness.

So how do you feel satisfied? A lot of it is reframing your perspective. Gratitude also helps, because it helps you to appreciate the things you do have in your life.

This is important because it means you'll start looking for more things to appreciate, and soon, you will feel appreciative. And that's one of the stepping stones toward happiness.

You have to learn how to be happy with yourself as is.

Being happy doesn't mean your life is going to be perfect, either. Life isn't perfect, and it's never going to be. You just learn how to deal with it and increase your resilience.

Being happy should just mean you're satisfied. It shouldn't be a mythical state of being that you're forever chasing.

You get to decide if you're happy or not. It's a conscious decision.

It's like stepping out of the shadows and into the light. Your entire world has gotten brighter, and you have high hopes.

Life is a lot like a video game. As you work through life, you continue to level up. But along the way, you face many obstacles and challenges. Every challenge makes you stronger.

The best part of playing a video game is *playing* it. You get joy from the adventure of the game, the same with life.

Finding Little Joys in The World

Gratitude for the little things is one of the best ways to find joy in your life. Many studies have documented the impact of gratitude on one's mental health. There are many benefits of practicing gratitude.

1. Your mental health improves the longer you practice gratitude.

2. When you practice gratitude, you experience more positive emotions.

3. You can experience the benefits of gratitude without sharing it with anyone.

4. Your medial prefrontal cortex shows greater neural sensitivity. This is the part of the brain responsible for learning and decision making.

5. You have better relationships with others.

6. You experience fewer pains and aches in your physical body.

7. You increase your mental well-being, with more positive emotions and fewer negative ones.

Finding Your Joy

Take some time to find play in your daily life. Do things that come easy to you and bring you joy. Figure out what joy looks like for you.

Does that look like:

- Painting?

- Writing?

- Dancing?

- Basketball?

- Cross country?

- Woodshop?

- Cooking?

Whatever it is, it's out there and it's waiting for you.

In Summary

Happiness isn't something you achieve. It's not a goal that you'll hit someday. You can learn how to be happy in the moment, and you can do that by doing things you love.

Next: how routine will help maintain your health

Chapter 12

Staying on Top of Your Health

After leaving the hospital, part of my recovery was getting a job. I was 27 and had never had a job in my entire life. I built my own business when I was 17, but I had difficulty with discipline. I had a shop on Etsy where I sold children's aprons and makeup bags. In spite of my success, I largely worked when I wanted to and had no real routine.

So, I got a job at Lowe's Foods working in the bakery. It gave me a routine and something to live for. It wasn't my dream job; I had no intention to stay there forever, but it provided a safe space for mc to recover. I worked in the morning and afternoon and soon developed a routine.

You need a routine to stabilize.

Why You Need a Routine

Other than a means of stabilization, there are many reasons to have a routine. Having a routine leads to better stress levels and improved mental health. It gives you more time to relax and less anxiety.

You will end up with a better sleep schedule and bedtime habits, which will improve your mental clarity. Sleeping well boosts your performance, emotional well-being, and energy level.

With a routine, you can make time to exercise and eat healthily. Whether you want to go for a run or to the gym, little habits like this go a long way. It will fuel your body and get you energized.

If you have a good routine, it's likely you will encourage others to do the same. You become the example that people follow. My favorite morning routine was when I:

- Woke up at 7 a.m.

- Meditated for 10 minutes

- Read for 30 minutes

- Went for a run

- Ate breakfast

Developing a good routine is especially important now that more people are working from home.

We still have to be disciplined enough to follow a routine. Without routine, we descend into chaos. Routine gives structure to our lives.

A routine provides a blueprint by which we abide. It frees us up from constant decision-making and lets us live more fulfilling lives.

Instead of being spontaneous and playing things by ear, set specific time aside to do certain things. It gives you what to do, when to do it, and where. Without it, we would all be stumbling around in the dark.

In bad times, my routine was more like "get up, forage for food, lock myself in my room, and watch TV."

It wasn't until I started my more structured morning routine that I felt like I was getting my life back together.

My Morning Routine

After I read *The Miracle Morning*, I was excited by the idea of morning routines. I thought it was an incredible opportunity to set up your day and change your life.

The whole premise was that you were setting time aside every morning to work on yourself and your goals, leading you to a more fulfilling life. I went full in.

Starting at 22 years old, every morning I got up, drank a glass of water, read a chapter of a book, and then I would lace up my shoes and go for a run. Running gave me endorphins, and I would always come home and feel the relief of a good run completed.

I did this even in the worst times.

When my dad died and my semester load was high, running gave me an outlet to deal with all of it.

I made sure to run on a regular basis. I even said (mostly to myself), "I'm no fun if I don't run."

Creating Your Own Routine

What worked for me doesn't necessarily mean the same thing works for you. I liked the simplicity of my morning routine because it followed a set schedule. What I liked about *The Miracle Morning* was that it gave a tried-and-true mechanism to set your own routine.

The author's routine set aside time for silence, affirmations, visualizing, exercising, reading, and writing. These six habits formed the cornerstones of a morning routine. Each one provides a necessary part of growth.

Your routine might look different than mine. You might like lifting weights, where I'm a runner.

Heck, you could do both. The point is that you create and maintain a routine.

I highly recommend having a morning routine. It's a powerful way to slowly change your life and set yourself up for success.

But, you'll have days when keeping a routine is difficult. That's when you need to lean on your routine even more.

In Summary

Know that you won't be perfect every day. You'll miss some days. What matters is that you don't let one day ruin the rest. If you have one bad day, don't let it become two. Wake up the next day and do better.

Routines are necessary to help you maintain sanity. They allow you stability and give you freedom.

Next: exploring alternative treatments for depression

Chapter 13

Alternative Treatments

After my psychotic break, I kept talking in circles, looping around and around. I was delusional, saying things that made no sense.

Despite all the doctors, hospitalizations, and medications, nothing worked. I needed something more.

I was introduced to electroconvulsive therapy. One of the psychiatrists we spoke to suggested it as a way to break my looping pattern. It was a scary concept we knew nothing about.

When I was admitted to the mental hospital for the third time, I started talking to my doctors about it. Back at home, my sister researched everything she could on the topic. The more we learned, the more comfortable we felt with it. It took a while before anything happened, but eventually, it did.

Electroconvulsive therapy (ECT)

Electroconvulsive therapy is a surgery where electrodes are placed on the patient's temple. While they are under, shockwaves are delivered to the brain to induce mini seizures. These seizures are designed to reset your neural pathways.

I started with an initial 12 sessions. ECT, for me, took place three times a week—Mondays, Wednesdays, and Fridays—and I did it every week for a month. The whole procedure only takes about 30 minutes.

Every few sessions, I took an assessment of my depression and anxiety levels.

The doctor then came in and talked to me about my symptoms. He kept asking, "Do you feel any depression?"

Twelve sessions went by, and I was still experiencing bouts of depression, so I signed on for another 12 sessions. All in all, I went through 24 sessions of ECT.

In the surgery room, I watched as they prepared for the treatment. They placed electrodes on my head and monitors on my chest.

They had a medical cocktail ready for injection. It was a sedative to put me to sleep and an anti-seizure drug to keep me from spasming.

The way they checked my progress was through my right big toe. They placed a blood pressure monitor around my ankle to halt the drug's effects.

The drugs entered my system and each time, for a moment, I was paralyzed with fear. I felt an instant of panic and wanted to tell them to stop, but I didn't.

The doctors spoke calmly, talking me through it, and sleep finally took over.

I didn't feel a single thing.

I was often tired after my sessions. Around session 16, I realized I wasn't feeling the weight of depression. By session 24, depression was a thing of the past.

Acupuncture

There are other methods you can try, too. One of the other methods I researched but didn't try was acupuncture. Acupuncture is an old Chinese medical practice where needles are inserted at specific points in the body. It's primarily used to treat physical pain, but has been used to treat other problems, such as depression.

Acupuncture has been used as a cure for many things, including:

- Low back pain

- Headaches

- Fibromyalgia

- Arthritis pain

- Carpal tunnel syndrome

- Dental pain

- Nausea

It may reduce the need for drugs and improve the quality of life for some with chronic pain. It rarely causes more than mild side effects.

Acupuncture is considered a "complementary" medicine that can be used in conjunction with other therapies.

In Summary

If you find you are resistant to medication or want to try something different, there are other treatment options out there. ECT is a powerful option, as well as acupuncture. Everybody will have their own treatment plan. It's about finding the one that works for you.

Conclusion

What's Next?

In the end, it all boils down to one thing: you have to be an active participant in your recovery. No amount of wishing or wanting will get you anywhere *unless you do the work.*

It's not going to happen overnight. It's going to take time. But you can take small steps every day to get closer. I'm not expecting you to change the world. I just want you to know you have the power to change *your* world.

You can't compare your journey to anybody else's. Everyone has a different journey. Don't get discouraged when it seems like you aren't making any progress. It's taken me far longer than a decade to even remotely feel like I've got my crap together.

RECOVERING FROM DEPRESSION

Journaling has been a large part of my recovery. I've put together a short list of journal prompts to start you on your own path.

1. What makes you feel powerful?

2. What are you most afraid of?

3. What do you want to do before you die?

4. If you knew you were going to die tomorrow, what would you want to do today?

5. What do you hope to achieve in the next five years?

6. What were you doing the last time you lost track of time?

7. What are your priorities in life?

8. What makes you feel really alive?

9. What don't you spend enough time doing?

10. How do you show love?

11. How do you cope when things go wrong?

12. How would you like to be remembered?

13. What helps you feel present and in the moment?

14. What can you do today that you couldn't a year ago?

15. What three changes can you make to live according to your personal values?

16. What do you value most in life?

17. List three personal beliefs you'd like to explore further.

18. How can you express self-love?

19. What habits would you like to give up?

20. What is one thing you can let go of?

Ultimately, it's up to you to decide how important your mental health is to you. How much do you want to get better? How much do you want to recover?

It sounds rough because it is. Nobody *wants* to be accountable. It's hard. Taking responsibility for your recovery will be one of the hardest things you've ever done. But, if you're ready and willing, you can do it.

You have the power.

The rest is on you.

Maggie Kelly is a writer who focuses on mental health and personal development. After a seventh grade course in biology, she became fascinated with genetics and what shapes a human. She decided to learn all about the human psyche and obtained her B.S. in Psychology.

Maggie has struggled with depression since her young teens. Her life trajectory changed after having a psychotic break and hitting rock bottom at 26. Following a 3-month stint in the mental hospital, she found the help she needed. She wrote this book to help others who also struggle with depression.

When not writing, you can find her singing and playing the guitar with her cats.

Love this book? Don't forget to leave a review!

Every review matters, and it matters a *lot!*

Head over to Amazon (or wherever you purchased this book) to leave an honest review for me.

I thank you endlessly.